Code and Courage

My Path to Agility and Leadership

PHOENIX
Publishing

Esther Mandina

Code and Courage: My Path to Agility & Leadership

Copyright © Esther Mandina 2025

First Edition

ISBN: 978-1-77928-421-1

Published by:

Phoenix Publishing
257 Swallow Road, Rynfield Benoni
1501, South Africa

phoenixconsultancy86@gmail.com

Code&Courage

My Path to Agility and Leadership

What others thought of this book

As technology threatens to outpace humanity, Code and Courage offers a vital recalibration. Esther Mandina reminds us that true leadership is not measured in velocity or metrics, but in presence, compassion, and truth. Through authentic reflections and hard-won insights, she redefines what leadership can look like in tech empathetic, adaptive, and rooted in purpose. This book is a must-read for anyone who's ever doubted their voice, questioned their path, or wondered if they belonged. Esther doesn't just show us how to lead she shows us how to live with conviction and compassion in every moment.

— April Wensel, Founder of Compassionate Coding

I've had the rare privilege of witnessing Esther's entire journey, from her earliest sparks of curiosity to her evolution into a bold, purpose-driven leader in the tech space. Watching her grow from dismantling gadgets at home to navigating complex Agile environments with empathy and clarity has been nothing short of inspiring. Over the past five years working alongside her, I've seen her turn challenges into catalysts and create spaces where people feel safe, seen and heard. Code & Courage isn't just a book; it's Esther in her purest form: thoughtful, honest and unwaveringly human. This is the kind of leadership the future needs and the kind of story that stays with you long after the final chapter.

— Olsen Mandina, Leadership & Technology Executive

An inspiring story of transformation from humble IT roots to an innovator driving real change. This is a must-read for future-focused IT professionals, aspiring leaders and innovators committed to driving change.

— Dr Theo Tsokota, Senior Lecturer

As someone who has had the privilege to mentor Esther in code, Code & Courage feels like the guide I wished I'd also had in my own journey starting out. Esther's journey from navigating the technical challenges of software development to mastering the human side of agility is inspiring. This book captures how true agility isn't just about delivering features faster, it's about showing up for your team when things get complicated, messy, or uncertain. Esther's stories reveal the power of courageous conversations and the kind of mentoring that transforms not only how we write code, but how we lead and support one another. Her blend of technical rigor with authentic empathy is rare. Whether she's deep in a code review or facilitating a difficult discussion, Esther embodies the principle that great software comes from brave teams who learn and grow together. This book is an essential reading for anyone who wants to become a better developer, mentor and teammate.

— Senior Software Developer & Mentor

Contents

Dedication

To the builders, the dreamers, the quiet disruptors — those who write code and rewrite their story at the same time. This book is for you.

Acknowledgements

This book was born of faith, fearlessness and the quiet courage to keep showing up.

To my family, who provided the constant runtime of love and belief even when the path felt uncertain.

To the mentors who showed me that leadership isn't about having all the answers—it's about asking the right questions.

To every team I've walked with, you are the source code of this journey. Your honesty, resilience, and brilliance shaped more than projects, you shaped me.

To my tech friends and fellow engineers there are too many to name, but each of you played a part. Thank you for walking this path with me, for the shared sprints, the late-night bug fixes, the deep debates, and the unwavering support. You made the hard parts lighter and the wins even brighter.

To Phoenix Publishing, thank you for backing this vision, for protecting its spirit, and for allowing it to breathe without compromise.

To the reader especially the one still visualizing possibility: you may doubt yourself, but keep building. Keep becoming. To code, you were never just a tool. You were a mirror, a lifeline, and an invitation to believe that broken systems internal or external can always be rebuilt. And finally, to the version of me who kept showing up, even when she wasn't sure how much further she could go: I'm proud of you. Keep showing up, even when unsure.

Foreword

Esther and I crossed paths while working at a global technology leader renowned not only for its telecommunications history, but also for pioneering innovations in network technology, software solutions, and emerging digital services. I am honored to write this foreword for such a remarkably talented and inspiring individual. Code and Courage: My Path to Agility and Leadership is far more than a book about technology — it's a tribute to the people who bring it to life. It explores those moments of doubt when you question your place and underscores the vital role mentors play in reminding us that we belong. Above all, it celebrates the bravery it takes to show up, even when fear is present.

As this book reveals, leadership isn't about being the loudest voice in the room; it's about genuine presence. It calls us to ask better questions, to stand at the edge of a big leap, and to find the courage to take that jump. It champions the power of collective intelligence and the agile values that sustain it. To be agile means embracing honesty — acknowledging when things are off track and accepting that as a starting point — because truth is the only way forward.

For me, leadership is the quiet courage to stand in uncertainty and take the next step anyway. It's the belief that every leap — no matter how small — creates ripples that inspire others to move too. When we lead with openness, agility becomes more than a framework; it becomes a way of life that invites others to bring their best selves forward.

The best leaders don't create followers; they create

more leaders. Leadership isn't about becoming someone new — it's about amplifying who you already are. This book is both a mirror and a map: a mirror reflecting the challenges we all face in leading with courage, and a map showing how agility can bridge the gap between where we are and where we aspire to be. My hope is that as you read, you'll find the courage to take your own leaps — and lead in ways that inspire others to do the same.

Ad Astra, always.

— Kelly Keodara

Founder and Chief Communications Strategist for *Earth & Space*

Introduction

"Hello, world." A simple rite of passage for programmers but for me, it marked the beginning of something far deeper than a technical career. For me, it was the start of a journey defined not just by lines of code, but leaps of faith. There were days filled with doubt and nights fueled by belief. I then started discovering that leadership isn't about having all the answers, it's about the courage to listen with intention.

When I first entered the world of technology, it was curiosity that sparked a fierce desire to figure out how things work. But it was courage that kept me going especially as the only lioness cub trying to prove to the pride that she could provide just as powerfully as her male counterparts in the tech jungle. I didn't feel ready for it. And sometimes, the toughest systems to debug aren't in the code, they're within ourselves.

A Passion Sparked Early

I wasn't the girl with the perfect tech setup. I was the girl borrowing my parents' laptop, opening Visual Basic and teaching herself to build forms one clumsy box at a time. I tore apart calculators just to see how they worked. My enthusiasm for technology blossomed during my university years, where I participated in coding competitions and collaborative projects with classmates. A friend, whose experience in programming far exceeded mine, played a big role in encouraging me not to give up on my academic journey. Those shared experiences and late night problem solving sessions solidified my desire to pursue a career in software engineering. That obsession with understanding systems became my foundation. It gave me a language I could control code in a world where many things felt out of my control.

And yet, the real breakthrough didn't come from coding.

It came from realizing that my work wasn't about the systems I built. It was about the people those systems served and the teams behind them

Entry into the Real World

When I landed my first software engineering role, I was excited and overwhelmed. I had the skills sure, but the environment was different. Real clients, real pressure and a silent weight of proving myself. I worked hard. I stayed late. I learned fast.

But I also felt isolated. I didn't see many people like me; a woman, young, ambitious, not always confident and that left a quiet ache. I kept wondering do I really belong here? Do I have what it takes for this role?

Then came the frustration not with the work itself, but with the way we were working. Rigid processes, delayed feedback and a constant rush that often missed the mark. I knew we could do better, and that curiosity led me to Agile.

Discovering Agile and Myself

Agile wasn't just a framework to me. It was a lifeline. A different way of thinking, one that made room for adaptation, collaboration and humanity.

I still remember the first time we ran a daily standup instead of a status report. I felt alive. We listened, we adjusted, and we connected. That project taught me something I never learned in university process matters, but people matter more.

That realization hit hard because up until that point, I was trying to survive in tech by blending in. Agile helped me lead by showing up as myself.

Becoming a Leader (Before I Felt Like One)

When I moved into Project Management and Scrum Master roles, it was terrifying. I didn't feel qualified to lead anything. But I said yes not because I was ready, but because I was willing to grow.

I have learned that leadership is often about that exact choice, showing up afraid and doing it anyway.

In those early days, I over prepared for every standup. I second guessed my decisions. I wrestled the imposter syndrome. But slowly, courage began to replace performance. I started facilitating conversations instead of controlling them. I began asking questions rather than pretending to have all the answers. And somewhere in that messy middle, I found my voice. Not the loudest in the room but steady, present and earned.

Over time, I began managing schedules and resources, initiating, delivering technical documentation and supporting complex team workflows across diverse environments. I facilitated retrospectives and team workshops, mentored others on Agile practices and helped teams embrace continuous improvement. I also contributed to broader program planning and quality milestones not just as a coordinator, but as a partner in building great outcomes.

These weren't just tasks. They were the building blocks of confidence. And today, whether I'm driving projects forward, supporting team dynamics or adapting to new tools and ways of working, I know leadership isn't about having all the answers, it's about growing into the kind of person who keeps showing up to ask better questions.

A Woman in Tech and in Leadership

Being a woman in tech still carries weight. There were moments I felt invisible and others when I felt scrutinized. I have been underestimated, talked over and left out of key decisions. But I've also learned that being **different** is my superpower.

My leadership is not loud, but it's intentional. It's rooted in empathy. I check in. I notice when people are struggling. I care about psychological safety because I've worked in environments where it didn't exist. That sensitivity, that awareness, comes from my journey and it shapes the kind of leader I choose to be.

A Pivotal Moment: When Everything Clicked

One project changed everything. Tight deadlines. Constant changes. High stakes. We embraced Agile principles and delivered not just on time, but beyond expectations. I got feedback from a senior stakeholder who said, *"We've never felt so heard, so involved."*

That stuck with me and that was the moment I realized Agile isn't about ceremonies, it's about connection. And leadership isn't about power, it's about presence.

Why I Wrote This Book

Code and Courage is not just a guide. It's a journey through the messy, beautiful and often vulnerable path of becoming. It's my way of saying you can lead without being perfect. You can pivot when you're scared. You can grow even when it feels like everything's falling apart.

In this book, I'll walk you through the principles that shaped my thinking, the tools that sharpened my skills, and the stories that shaped my soul. You'll hear the lessons I learned the hard way. You'll also find letters to my younger self and maybe to yours, too.

So, if you've ever felt like an outsider in tech, if you've ever doubted your ability to lead, or if you're standing at the edge of a big leap…I hope this book gives you the nudge you need to jump with courage.

End of Chapter Reflections:

Pull Quote:

"Leadership doesn't always look like certainty. Sometimes, it looks like showing up anyway shaky hands and all."

Journal Prompt:

Recall a moment when you felt like an outsider in your career or life. What did you tell yourself then? What do you wish someone had told you?

Reflection Corner

1

Hello Leadership, My First Real Commit

(From the lens of a woman learning to lead with purpose and heart)

My journey of a thousand lines began with Hello World.

I didn't know it then, but those early keystrokes would teach me more than syntax, they'd show me how to rebuild myself, line by line, especially when life refused to compile.

For years, I thought leadership would be about titles, positions, or recognition. I thought my value was in how many lines of code I wrote or how many bugs I fixed. But leadership revealed itself to me in unexpected ways — in moments of doubt, in mistakes, and in the quiet courage it took to show up anyway.

I didn't truly understand Agile until I was forced to.

It was during a project that felt like it was unraveling by the hour. Deadlines missed, team members' morale dropping and progress obscured by noise. I remember sitting in yet another meeting, surrounded by static reports and rigid planning artifacts that no longer reflected the reality on the ground. That's when I asked the question out loud:

"What if there's a better way?"

It felt like trying to refactor a broken function while

the program was still running, messy, urgent, but necessary.

That wasn't just a question about process, it was a turning point in how I thought about leadership, teamwork and growth. A recognition that effectiveness in complex environments isn't about tighter control but about smarter adaptability.

I remember one of my earliest leadership moments: I had been asked, unexpectedly, to lead a sprint planning meeting. Fresh out of school, the youngest in the room, I wanted to hide behind my laptop and let the seniors talk. But something inside me whispered, "You've been given this role for a reason. Own it." My voice shook as I began outlining the goals for the sprint. At first, the faces staring back at me were skeptical. But halfway through, one of the senior developers leaned forward and said, "That actually makes sense." That moment taught me that leadership often begins not with confidence, but with courage. It was my first real commit — not to GitHub, but to showing up as a leader.

Another lesson came late one night during a deployment. Everything looked good until 2 a.m., when the build failed. My stomach dropped. My first thought was, "I'm done. I've ruined everything." I had two choices: stay silent and hope no one noticed, or own it and call for help. It took courage to choose the second option, but to my surprise, my lead didn't scold me. Instead, he said, "Good leaders don't hide problems. They surface them fast." That moment reshaped my understanding of leadership: courage isn't never failing. Courage is owning failure before it owns you.

Agile and Project Management wasn't new to me in theory. I had studied the frameworks, values, read the books and even passed the certifications. But knowing Agile is one thing. Living it, trusting it when everything feels unstable is something else entirely. It's one thing to write a clean backlog, it's another to deploy under pressure, manage live updates and keep your mental stack from overflowing.

And to be honest, I didn't feel **Agile** at all at first. I felt uncertain, stretched and afraid I'd let people down. It was like debugging in production, no time for perfection, only for presence.

But that's where this journey really began.

Agile As A Mindset — Not Just A Method

People often think of Agile as sticky notes on whiteboards, sprints, retrospectives and user stories. But for me, Agile started showing up in my **personal mindset** before it ever changed my work practices. It showed up when I gave myself permission to iterate, to grow in public and to not have it all figured out. It felt like versioning myself. Each step a small release, with feedback loops built in. And like any codebase, I had to learn to accept pull requests from others. It showed up when I asked for feedback, not as criticism but as collaboration.

It showed up in quiet moments, like staying late to prepare for a sprint planning meeting and realizing I'm not just managing tasks. I'm holding space for people.

Agile gave me a new language for leadership one rooted in empathy, adaptability and trust.

I often think of leadership the way I think about Git. A commit is local, a private decision. A push is public, something others can see. Leadership works the same way. The first commit is always to yourself — the decision to step up even when no one else is watching. The second commit is to your team, the willingness to show up for others, even when you feel uncertain. The third commit is to growth — the courage to remain a learner. Only when you "push" do others see it, but it is courage that bridges the gap between the private commit and the public action.

The First Time I Facilitated A Retrospective

I was nervous.

Everyone was looking at me, waiting for direction. I had planned out the **start, stop, continue** board, set up the Whiteboard links and practiced my prompts. But what I didn't plan for was silence.

It felt like a command waiting for input, a terminal blinking, and a frozen cursor, waiting for someone to type the first line of courage. That awkward silence when no one wanted to speak first. I panicked inside *"They're not engaged… I've failed… I'm not meant for this role."*

But then, I remembered something my mentor once said:

"When you're unsure, lead with a question instead of a statement."

So I took a breath, smiled and said, *"What's one small thing that made your day easier this week?"*

It wasn't magic, but it opened the loop and slowly, the room started to run again. One team member spoke up. Then another. And soon, we were in a deep, meaningful conversation not just about tasks, but about trust. About how we were feeling.

That was the day I truly understood Agile isn't about speeding up. It's about *showing up*. It's like optimizing not for throughput, but for clarity. Not how fast the function runs, but whether it's doing what really matters.

There were many other *firsts*. The first time I told a client, "I don't know, but I'll find out." That simple admission built more credibility than pretending to know ever could. The first time my pull request was rejected in review — I felt crushed until the reviewer told me, "I'm not rejecting you. I'm helping you level up." I realized feedback is code review for the soul. It stings, but it grows you.

What Agile Taught Me About Myself

Before Agile, I measured my worth by how much I could *do*. After Agile, I started measuring my impact by how well I could listen.

I stopped trying to fix everything alone and started believing in the power of collective intelligence. I learned that my role wasn't to have all the answers, but to ask better questions. To guide conversations, to promote psychological safety and to empower others to rise.

And as a woman in tech, that shift was liberating.

I didn't have to lead like anyone else. I could lead like *me*.

Not every system needs the same architecture. I stopped trying to follow someone else's blueprint and started trusting the logic I was learning to write for myself.

I learned this lesson in unexpected places. Once, during testing, a bug appeared in a module I hadn't touched. I could have said, "Not my fault." Instead, I stepped in to help trace it. Together, the team fixed it. Later, my manager said, "You acted like a leader." Leaders don't protect their egos. They protect the system. Another time, in a meeting with executives, silence fell after a difficult question. I wanted to shrink, but instead I spoke, offering a small observation. The VP nodded and said, "That's insightful." That day I learned that your voice matters, even if it shakes.

Through all these moments, I came to understand the difference between courage and confidence. Confidence is the assurance built over time. Courage is the step you take before confidence shows up. Most leadership firsts — the first presentation, the first mistake, the first "I don't know" — feel terrifying. But courage creates the history that builds confidence.

The Core Agile Values — Through My Lens

Let me share what these values really mean to me not just as principles, but as anchors I return to when I feel overwhelmed:

1. Collaboration

I used to think asking for help was a weakness. Now I know it's a superpower.

Agile taught me that the best outcomes happen together. We co-create, we co-learn and that's how trust is built.

I remember once working with a junior developer who barely spoke in meetings. She had brilliant ideas but kept them to herself.

During one sprint review, I asked her directly, "What do you think?" Her suggestion ended up solving a problem that had blocked us for days.

That moment changed how I saw collaboration — it isn't just about dividing tasks. It's about making space for hidden voices to be heard. That's how trust deepens, line by line, like carefully written code that only becomes powerful when integrated with the rest of the system.

2. Flexibility

Agile invited me to surrender control in the best way. When plans change and they always do, I no longer see it as failure. I see it as evolution.

One release cycle, a vendor outage delayed everything. The old version of me would have spiraled into panic. But Agile taught me to pivot.

Instead of obsessing over the missed deadline, I asked the team, "What can we learn from this?" We ended up redesigning part of the workflow to make it more resilient.

Flexibility, I realized, isn't about abandoning plans — it's about having the courage to rewrite them when reality shifts. It's evolution in motion.

3.   Continuous Improvement

This one hit deep. I've had weeks where I cried after a daily stand up meeting because I felt I hadn't done enough. But Agile taught me that we improve in increments. One better conversation. One better decision. One kinder self-reflection. Even in code, the best features start as pull requests. Progress doesn't need to be perfect — just pushed forward.

The same holds true in leadership. Once, after a tense retrospective, I went home feeling like I'd failed the team. But when I looked back, I realized we had still inched forward. We had learned, argued honestly, and emerged clearer than before. Improvement isn't always visible sprint by sprint.

Sometimes it's hidden, like background processes running silently until one day, the system feels faster and lighter. Leadership, like code, improves through many small commits, not one grand release.

4.   Customer Focus

Sometimes the "customer" isn't a client, it's the team. It's the person who's too quiet to speak up, or too burnt out to finish the sprint. Leading with empathy means asking, *"Who are we really building for?"*

I once thought *"customer focus"* meant making clients happy at all costs. But Agile shifted my view. The real "customer" is anyone affected by the system. Once, during a crunch period, I noticed a teammate staying late every night. Instead of praising the hustle, I asked if he was okay. He admitted he was close to burnout. We restructured workloads, and the project moved forward more sustainably. That day I learned: customer focus starts with the humans right in front of you. The code doesn't run if the coders burn out.

The Courage To Shift The Culture

- Agile isn't just something you do. It's something You embody.

- It takes courage to challenge outdated ways of working.

- It takes vulnerability to say, "Let's try something different."

- It's like rewriting core logic without knowing if it will compile but trusting the output will be worth it.

- It takes resilience to keep going when the room is resistant.

But when it clicks, when the team starts humming, when the backlog reflects real needs, when retrospectives feel honest there's nothing like it.

That's when I know: this is worth it.

It takes courage to reach that point. Courage to ask the harder questions. Courage to admit when something isn't working. Courage to believe that culture isn't just the responsibility of executives or HR, but of every person who contributes to the system.

Micro-Courage: The Building Blocks Of Culture

Big acts of courage get attention, but it's the smaller, everyday choices that build lasting culture. I call them "micro-courage." It's the teammate who says, "I need help" instead of struggling silently. It's the leader who pauses a meeting to ask, "How are you, really?" It's the engineer who reviews code with kindness as well as clarity. None of these moments make headlines. But together, they create the psychological safety that allows teams to thrive.

Micro-courage is like unit testing. A single test might not seem significant, but thousands of small tests layered together make the whole system resilient. Without them, the codebase becomes brittle. Without micro-courage, culture becomes fragile.

Three Signals of a Courageous Culture

Looking back, I've noticed three signals that tell me when a team is shifting toward a healthier culture:

First, honesty in retrospectives. When people stop sugarcoating and begin to tell the truth about what's working and what isn't, it means they trust the room enough to be real.

Second, safety in dissent. True agility isn't about everyone nodding in agreement. It's about disagreement handled with respect. A team that can argue fiercely without fracturing is a team that can grow.

And third, visible empathy. Not empathy spoken about in values statements, but empathy practiced in real-time: someone stepping in to help a struggling colleague, someone giving credit generously, someone choosing patience over frustration. These are the quiet proofs that courage has taken root.

Agility isn't just about changing how we work; it's about changing how we show up when everything feels uncertain. That's what makes it sustainable — not the stickies, not the ceremonies, but the culture of courage behind them.

End of Chapter Reflections:

Pull Quote:

"Agility isn't just about changing how we work; it's about changing how we show up when everything feels uncertain."

Journal Prompt:

Think of a moment when you felt uncertain in your work but chose to show up anyway. What helped you push through?

What did you learn about yourself?

What one courageous choice could you make this week that would ripple into your team's culture?

Reflection Corner

2

Why Code Alone Isn't Enough – Developing People Skills in Tech

I used to think my code would speak for itself. If I worked hard enough, stayed late enough, fixed enough bugs, someone would notice. That I didn't have to talk much, I just had to deliver.

But here's the thing they don't always tell you in tech:

- **Code can open the door, but people skills will keep you in the room.**

And I learned that the hard way.

When Code Wasn't Enough

I remember one project early in my career the specs were tight, the deadline tighter. I gave everything to that codebase. Sleepless nights. Endless testing. I even skipped family celebrations just to push features over the finish line.

When we launched, it worked beautifully. But the client wasn't thrilled. Not because the code failed, but they felt unheard throughout the process. They had changes, they never communicated clearly and I never asked.

That was my wake up call.

Tech is about humans not just machines. Even the most elegant code can fail if the inputs are wrong. I learned the same goes for people, if we don't ask the right questions, we won't get the right outcomes.

If I could write a script for the version of me that grew from this — it might look something like below. It wouldn't be optimized for speed. It would be structured for empathy, error-handled for burnout, and flexible enough to grow with real world inputs.

```
// 1. Embrace uniqueness
if (isDifferent(self)) {
    stayStrong();
}

// 2. Upgrade to leader mode
self.upgrade(version = "2.0");    // Becoming a leader

// 3. Handle crises gracefully
try {
    runMission();
} catch (Exception e) {
    handleCrisis(e);
}

// 4. Lead from within
return authenticity();    // Leading from within
```

This wasn't about code anymore. It was about courage, growth and choosing to lead differently.

It was about learning that systems can scale, but trust must be earned. That your voice matters as much in a planning meeting as it does in a pull request. That leadership isn't declared; it's practiced in moments of clarity, conflict and care.

And above all, it was about realizing:

You don't have to be the loudest or the most technical to lead. You just have to be human and brave enough to keep iterating on who you're becoming.

The Moment I Learned To Listen

This day changed everything. A junior team member had gone quiet for a few days. Normally chatty, suddenly withdrawn. I could've ignored it, chalked it up to mood.

But I paused and said, *"You okay? You seem a little off.*

Want to talk?"

He hesitated, then opened up about burnout, stress at home and feeling like he wasn't contributing enough. I listened. I didn't try to fix it right away. I just held the space.

He later told me, "That conversation saved me from quitting in tech."

That day, I understood the power of presence. Not presence in the room but *presence with people.*

Listening became one of the most underrated skills in my toolkit. When it comes to code, a semicolon misplaced can unravel code; while in life, a moment unheard unravel trust.

I've been on the other side too. There was a time I was silently burning out, convinced I had to "hold it together." When a mentor asked me one simple question — "How are you really?" — it cracked something open. I learned that sometimes the courage to ask is as life-changing as the courage to answer

From Soft Skills To Power Skills

People often call them "soft" skills as if they're optional. But I've come to see them as *power* skills:

Communication: Knowing when to speak, when to listen and how to say hard things with kindness.

There was a sprint where I over-explained everything in technical jargon. My non-technical stakeholders nodded politely, but later admitted they understood nothing. The project veered off course.

That's when I realized communication isn't about proving how much you know — it's about ensuring others feel confident enough to engage. Clear communication is inclusive; it bridges worlds

Emotional intelligence: Reading the room. Managing your own triggers. Responding, not reacting.

Conflict resolution: Staying grounded in difficult conversations instead of shutting down or lashing out.

I once witnessed two engineers arguing fiercely over architecture choices. I felt tempted to avoid the tension. But instead, I reframed the debate: "What's the problem we're actually solving?" Suddenly the heat dropped, and the focus returned to the customer. Conflict is inevitable; escalation isn't. Leaders don't eliminate conflict — they channel it into growth.

Empathy: Seeing beyond the ticket number or user story to the human being on the other side.

These aren't just nice to have. They're game changers. Especially for those of us trying to lead, mentor or break barriers in a world not always built for us.

The Confidence To Speak Up

There was a time I doubted everything I said in meetings. I'd script talking points, rehearse responses, then shrink back anyway when the moment came. I thought everyone else was smarter, louder and more "qualified" to lead.

But leadership doesn't always look like certainty. Sometimes it looks like showing up *even when your voice shakes*.

The first time I challenged a design decision in a client call, my heart was pounding. But I spoke from experience, not ego. I offered a different perspective and to my surprise, the client leaned in.

"You're right," he said. "That makes a lot more sense."

That moment reminded me, your voice matters not

despite who you are, but *because* of who you are.

Since then, I've had other firsts. The first time I led a demo. The first time I presented to executives. The first time I said, "I don't agree." Every time, my voice shook. Every time, courage showed up before confidence did.

Silence in a meeting is like untested code. It hides potential problems until they become production bugs. Speaking up isn't just about being heard; it's about protecting the integrity of the system.

Mentorship That Changed My Trajectory

One of my greatest blessings was a mentor who saw what I didn't see in myself.

He once told me *"You can code with the best of them, but your real superpower is how you bring people together."*

That stuck. Because I had spent so much time trying to "prove" I belonged in tech through code; I had forgotten that my presence, my intuition and my *people lens* were just as needed.

Now, as a mentor myself, I try to be that mirror for others, especially young people entering tech unsure if they fit. I often tell them, "You don't have to sound like anyone else. You just have to sound like *you*. And that's more than enough."

Over the years, I began to realize that leadership in tech isn't a title you wear, but a set of principles you return to again and again. They aren't written in code, but they run in the background of every decision, every conversation, every line of trust built with others. These became the lessons I now live by — not as theories, but as practices earned through mistakes, failures, and small acts of courage.

Lessons I Now Live By

- Ask before assuming.
- Listen with your whole body.
- Celebrate team wins louder than your own.
- Stay curious, not judgmental.
- Kindness is not weakness.

These lessons may seem simple, almost obvious, but they are deceptively hard to practice under pressure. Asking before assuming takes humility. Listening with your whole body takes presence. Celebrating team wins louder than your own takes generosity. Staying curious requires resisting the easy comfort of judgment. Lastly, kindness especially in a world that often mistakes sharpness for strength — takes tremendous courage. They are not just leadership habits; they are survival skills for building cultures that last.

Because in the world of tech where deadlines loom and logic reigns, emotional awareness becomes a quiet revolution. In tech, we test our code before we deploy it. Maybe we should start testing our listening the same way with empathy as the compiler.

End of Chapter Reflections:

Pull Quote:

"Code builds systems. But people skills build cultures."

Journal Prompt:

Think of a moment when you felt truly seen or heard by someone at work. What did they do that made a difference? What would it look like to debug a culture not with code, but with compassion?

How can you offer that to someone else?

Reflection Corner

3

Tools and Techniques for New and Aspiring Agile Practitioners

I used to believe that mastery came from knowing all the tools. The dashboards, the metrics, the processes but what I've learned is this: **the real tools of leadership are invisible.**

They're called self-awareness, trust, intuition and timing.

And yes, Jira is helpful. So is Trello. But the most powerful tool I've ever used as a Scrum Master... is *a question asked at the right moment.*

My First Agile Toolkit... And My First Mistake

I remember walking into my first official sprint planning meeting armed with everything I'd read online. My Jira board was flawless. The user stories were neatly organized. My estimation technique time boxed to the minute.

But the team was *checked out.*

People nodded, but no one engaged. We finished early not because we were efficient, but because we avoided the real conversation.

That day taught me something that had no certification and that **tools wouldn't fix culture.**

You can have the perfect setup but if people don't feel safe, heard or valued, the tools will gather dust.

Looking back, I realize I had fallen into practicing what I now call cargo cult Agile — following the ceremonies but missing the mindset behind them. Just as a code snippet copied from Stack Overflow won't solve your unique problem unless you understand it, no tool will transform a team unless it's grounded in trust and purpose.

The Tools I Use — And How I Use Them *With Heart*

Here's a more honest look at the tools I still use today but through the lens of *connection, not control.*

- **Jira**

Yes, it's great for backlog grooming, tracking velocity, and sprint planning. But what I love most is using it during retrospectives. We pull up the board and ask together:

"Does this feel realistic?" "Is anything draining us?"

It becomes less about data, and more about dialogue. Once, I noticed our velocity looked stable — yet the team's energy felt off. By surfacing that mismatch, we discovered hidden burnout. Without that conversation, the numbers would've lied.

- **Trello / Notion**

I've used these for visual collaboration, especially with newer or non-technical teams. I once used Trello to map a team's learning journey across an internal bootcamp.

Watching their confidence grow as they moved cards from "confused" to "crushing it" was beautiful. The board became less of a tracker and more of a celebration wall.

- ### Slack / MS Teams

Beyond updates and check-ins, these tools became my virtual empathy space. One day, a junior developer pinged me on Slack:

"Can I be honest? I'm overwhelmed. I don't want to slow down the sprint."

We jumped on a quick call, re-prioritized tasks, and gave her space. She finished strong. Agile isn't just about *delivering fast, it's about responding with care.*

- ### ClickUp /Monday

These tools thrive when complexity grows. At some point I've used them to bring clarity to chaos especially when leading cross-functional teams juggling multiple deliverables and shifting priorities.

What I appreciate most isn't just the features, it's the visibility. ClickUp and Monday help everyone see how their work ladders up to the bigger picture.

When someone asks, *"Where do I start?"* or *"Why does this matter?"* — these tools become maps, not just boards.

- ### Confluence

Documentation isn't just for developers. I use Confluence as our shared memory. It's where lessons live, where decisions are recorded and where people go when I'm not around.

During one major release, we hit a wall. Confusion spread. And then someone quietly said, *"Wait, didn't we solve this six months ago?"*

They searched, found the old decision document and we moved forward. No Slack thread could've done that.

That's when I realized: ***Documentation is leadership in written form.***

- **Power BI**

Leadership isn't just instinct it's, insight. I turn to Power BI when I need to step back and ask:

Where are we trending? Are we stuck or just tired?
Which assumptions need a second look?

It's not about micromanaging metrics. It's about recognizing patterns, seeing the invisible, and making better decisions with compassion, not just calculation.

Tools Are Temporary, Impact Is Lasting

Of course, the tools I use today may not be the ones I use tomorrow. Platforms evolve. Teams shift. New solutions emerge. What matters isn't staying loyal to a brand, it's staying loyal to the **needs of your people** and the **values of your leadership**.

Whether it's **Jira or something that hasn't been invented yet**, the real question I keep asking is: *"Does this tool help us connect, grow and deliver better together?"*

Because in the end, tools are just instruments.

What makes them powerful is the **intention behind them**.

These tools help me lead with both **structure and soul**.

They remind me that behind every task is a person, and behind every metric is a moment that mattered. They help me serve, listen, adapt, and deliver with care.

The tools may change.

But the heart of how I use them **stays the same**.

Looking ahead to the future, I imagine teams will work with tools we can barely picture today. When AI copilots draft user stories for us or virtual retrospectives that will take places in immersive virtual spaces. The truth will still hold: tools don't make leaders. **Leaders make tools meaningful.**

The Techniques That Shaped My Growth

I've experimented with many Agile techniques, some flopped, some flourished but a few became staples in my leadership toolkit, not because they were fancy but because they invited honesty.

- **User Stories That Feel Like Real Life**

"As a user, I want X…"

That structure is great, but I always challenge teams to add one more question:

"What pain is this solving?"

That one line changes the conversation from task focused to impact driven. Once, during a product workshop, asking this question stopped a whole feature from being built, saving weeks of work — because we realized it wasn't solving a real problem. Sometimes, subtraction is the bravest form of delivery.

- **Planning Poker but Make It Fun**

We once renamed estimation points as animals. A "3," became a Turtle 🐢, slow but doable. A "13," was an elephant, huge, heavy 🐘. The room lit up. Laughter entered.

People started explaining their reasoning more freely. It reminded me that Agile doesn't have to be dry. It can be *human, playful and alive*

❖ Retrospectives That Heal

During one retrospective, I asked:

❖ *"What's one thing you wish someone noticed in this sprint but didn't?"*

That simple question opened a floodgate. A tester admitted feeling invisible. A developer admitted to burnout.

We didn't solve everything, but we saw each other and that's what retros are really for.

My Realest Tool? Courage.

Being a leader isn't just sticky notes and schedules. It's knowing when to pause a meeting to check on someone's body language. It's being brave enough to say, "we are off track and that's okay."

One of my proudest moments was during a cross functional workshop. Tension was high. Deadlines were looming. Everyone was defending their turf.

I interrupted and said,

"Let's stop. What's really going on here?"

Silence.

Then one voice broke it:

"We're all just scared. We want this to succeed... and we're afraid to fail." That moment realigned the whole project.

Agile isn't about tools. Agile is about **truth.**

The Innovation Award: The Spark I Almost Ignored

I almost deleted the email. "Nominated for Innovation Award?" I thought it was a mistake. I didn't even know someone had noticed my work, let alone value it that highly. I wasn't sure if I deserved it. But that nomination changed something in me.

I didn't wake up that morning expecting anything life changing. I was just trying to survive my calendar packed with meetings, follow ups and backlogged action items. Our company was hosting a global innovation showcase and I honestly had no plans to attend. My plate was too full.

It was my manager who nudged me. "Just take a quick walk with me," he said. "Let's go see what's happening at the event."

We wandered past booths filled with flashy demos and pitch decks. Then we stumbled on the Innovation Booth, a space where employees could submit ideas for improving internal workflows. Half, jokingly, my manager said, "Esther, you always have creative ideas why don't you drop one in?"

I hesitated. I almost brushed it off. But something clicked. That very week, I'd been wrestling with inefficiencies in some operations that were slowing everything down. And I thought, *What if we could use Artificial Intelligence (AI) to fix this?*

So, I wrote it down nothing fancy, just raw and real. A use case for applying machine learning to solve a real bottleneck. I submitted it and went back to work, honestly forgetting about it.

A few weeks later, an email popped up.

"Congratulations, Esther. Your idea has been selected for this year's Company's Innovation Award."

I froze. Read it again. Then again.

A few weeks later, I was on a stage at the Innovation Award Ceremony. Flash bulbs. Applause. And a moment of disbelief that this idea born out of one ordinary moment could be seen, celebrated and *implemented*.

That day everything changed not because of the trophy, but because of the reminder **every overlooked idea holds power.**

How I Stay Sharp And Humble

I still reread *Scrum: The Art of Doing Twice the Work in Half the Time*. But I also read *Dare to Lead* by Brené Brown because vulnerability is a Scrum value too.

I join Agile meet-ups not to "network," but to sit in a room where I'm reminded, I'm not alone.

I ask for feedback even when it stings. Because growth doesn't always feel good but it's always worth it.

And I keep a journal of my leadership "bugs and fixes" — moments I got it wrong, and how I'll refactor next time. Just like code, leadership improves through commits, reviews and iterations.

End of Chapter Reflections:

Pull Quote:

"The most powerful Agile tool isn't a board. It's brave, honest conversation."

Journal Prompt:

Think of a time you used a tool, a presentation, a process, a framework and it didn't land.

What was missing beneath the surface?

How could empathy have changed the outcome?

Ask your team this week: *"Which tool feels heavy, and which one feels freeing?"* Listen more than you speak.

Reflection Corner

4

Embracing Leadership – Beyond Coding and Into Courage

I didn't set out to become a leader.

For a long time, I thought I would always be "the builder." The one behind the code, behind the delivery board and behind the solution. But somewhere between late night bug fixes and morning standups, I realized something:

I wasn't just managing tasks, I was shaping how people worked, how they felt and how they grew.

At first, I resisted it. I was trained in the comfort of logic. Leadership felt like stepping into unstructured territory. But the further I leaned in, the more I saw that the future of tech and Agile wasn't about hierarchy. It was about humanity.

From Agile Scripts To Real Human Leadership

In the early days, I followed the Agile script to the letter, daily standups, burndown charts, retrospectives, definitions of done. It worked. Until it didn't.

Teams evolved. Projects grew messier. People started asking for *more;* not just speed and efficiency, but flexibility, empathy and meaning. It became clear: **Agile wasn't the destination, it was the doorway.**

I had to lead beyond the roles. Beyond Scrum Master, beyond Project Manager. I had to lead as *myself*; adaptive, emotionally aware and grounded in purpose.

There's a moment I'll never forget. A developer and a tester were locked in conflict over a defect. The room was thick with tension. All eyes turned to me. The "script" said to escalate. But something told me to pause. I asked a simple question:

"What outcome do we both care about?"

That question broke the ice. They realized they weren't enemies — they were allies chasing the same goal. That was the day I learned leadership isn't about having the right process; it's about creating the right space.

When I Outgrew My Keyboard

It didn't happen all at once. At first it was small things.

I'd find myself asking questions in meetings that others weren't about... stakeholder goals, about team morale and about delivery impact.

While others focused on commits, I found myself focused on clarity.

But I also doubted myself constantly. "Am I leaving tech behind?"

"Will people still respect me if I'm not pushing code?" "Who do I think I am, calling myself a leader?"

Still, something inside me whispered, *"Keep going."*

And I'm so glad I did.

Because what I eventually realized is this: my ability to code gave me access. My ability to connect gave me influence.

Leading in the PostAgile Era

Let's talk about the real world. The now. Because post Agile leadership is here and it's reshaping everything.

- ### The Role of AI in Team Workflows

Artificial Intelligence isn't replacing leadership, it's enhancing it. Tools like ChatGPT and automation bots help streamline reports, draft documentation and even generate daily summary standups. But here's the truth: Artificial Intelligence can draft words, but it cannot discern the silence in someone's tone. It cannot sense when a "yes" really means "I'm drowning."

As a leader, I now spend less time coordinating and more time coaching. Less time managing tasks, more time managing trust. AI doesn't make leaders obsolete. It makes human presence indispensable.

- ### Dashboards that Support Emotional Intelligence

Metrics matter but what they reflect matters more. Modern dashboards aren't just about velocity or throughput. They're about *team health*.

We track mood check ins. Burnout indicators. Workload balance. Data becomes a mirror for emotional patterns.

Because emotional intelligence isn't separate from performance, it *drives* it. A tired team doesn't innovate. A burned-out team doesn't sustain success.

- ### From Fixed Roles to Fluid Collaboration

In the post, Agile era, roles like Project Manager, Scrum Master or Product Owner aren't only job, titles they're hats we wear when needed.

One week I'm facilitating. The next, I'm strategizing. The next, I'm mentoring a junior developer through burnout.

Leadership now means *flexibility without fragmentation. The future belongs to leaders who can shift seamlessly between builder, coach, strategist and servant leader.*

- **Leading Across Borders and Timezones**

With hybrid and distributed workforces, leadership now spans cultures, continents and timezones. I've led meetings at midnight for one team and at dawn for another. I've seen silence in one culture mean respect, and in another mean disengagement. Post-Agile leadership requires cultural fluency — not assuming one model works everywhere, but adapting like code refactored for different systems.

- **The Rise of Ethical Tech Leadership**

Soon, leaders won't just be judged on delivery, but on ethics. Did your AI exclude certain voices? Did your product respect privacy? Did you prioritize sustainability? These aren't side conversations anymore. They are central to leadership.

Practical Leadership Toolkit

Here are five techniques I use to lead with both vision and heart in this new digital landscape:

1. **Data Driven Decision Making**

Gut instincts are powerful, but data gives one perspective.

Before I change a process or intervene with a team, I look at trends:

Are we overcommitting every sprint? Are blockers recurring in a pattern? Data is a compass. But wisdom is knowing when to follow it and when to listen to the unspoken stories behind it.

2. Emotional Intelligence in the Age of Automation

Just because AI can generate a team update doesn't mean it should replace a real check in.

I still open retros with human moments: *"What was your energy like this week?"*

Soft data is still *data*. And emotional tone tells me more than a Gantt chart ever could.

3. Continuous Learning and Adaptability

The tools will change. The frameworks will evolve.

But if I'm always learning, I'm never behind.

Whether it's a new AI assistant, a behavioral model or a conflict resolution method, curiosity keeps me relevant.

4. Collaboration Between Humans and Machines

I train teams to see AI as a *collaborator*, not a threat.

We automate backlog grooming suggestions, run idea sessions with AI support and offload routine tasks so our creativity can thrive.

Machines give us efficiency. We give ourselves empathy. Together, that's where the future of work lies.

5. Inclusive Leadership in a Diverse Digital World

With remote, hybrid and global teams inclusivity is no longer optional.

I design meetings for different time zones, use visual tools for neurodiverse thinkers and ensure all voices, especially the quiet ones are heard.

Real leadership reflects the *whole team*, not just the

loudest.

Imposter Syndrome In A New Role

When I became a Scrum Master and later a Project Manager, I felt like I was walking around in a jacket two sizes too big. I kept waiting for someone to say, *"Who let her in here?"*

But something surprising happened.

People didn't want me to be perfect. They wanted me to be present.

To listen. To own mistakes. To care.

I've learned leadership isn't about knowing everything.

It's about creating spaces where people feel safe enough to be great.

The Identity Shift

Letting go of "coder" as my main identity was hard. Coding had been my safe zone, my badge of legitimacy.

But I slowly realized:

My ability to code gave me access.
My ability to connect gave me influence.

Now, as a project leader, I don't just deploy software, I build systems of trust. I align people, I break down silos and I amplify unheard voices.

And honestly? That impact feels even more powerful than deploying a perfect script.

The Moments That Changed Me

- **The day a stakeholder said, *"You make things feel less chaotic."***

  I realized calm is part of my leadership currency.

- **The time I admitted in a retrospective, *"I missed something. That's on me."***

  The team leaned in with more respect not less.

- **When I coached someone into *their* first Leadership role.**

  That was a full circle moment. Empowering others is how I know I'm on the right path.

The Courage To Say "Yes" Before You're Ready

I didn't become a leader when I got a title.

I became a leader the moment I said yes to growth even when I felt under qualified.

There's a lie we tell ourselves in tech that leadership is reserved for the confident, the assertive, the ones who "look the part."

But leadership can look like quiet resolve. Like late night preparation. Like learning out loud. It can look like *you* exactly as you are evolving.

Your Path Might Look Different And That's Okay

You don't have to follow a traditional ladder.

You can step into Agile coaching, product ownership, people management or even carve your own hybrid role.

What matters is not your title, it's your *trajectory*.

Are you growing? Are you contributing with purpose? Are you lifting others as you climb?

If the answer is yes, you're already leading.

End of Chapter Reflections:

Pull Quote:

"You don't grow into leadership by having all the answers. You grow into it by saying yes to the unknown."

Journal Prompt:

When was the last time you said yes to something that scared you?

What did that experience teach you about your own strength or potential?

Reflection Corner

5

Empowering the Next Generation – Advice for Aspiring Tech Professionals

Sometimes I think about the younger version of me hunched over a laptop, surrounded by fear and possibility.

Hungry to learn. Terrified to fail.

Wondering, *"Is there space for someone like me in tech?"*

The answer I've discovered over the years is a resounding yes. But not because someone handed me a roadmap, because I chose to keep showing up. And now? I want to be that roadmap for someone else.

If you're just getting started in tech, I hope this chapter feels like a friend. A voice saying, *"You've got this and you don't have to do it alone!"*

You Don't Need Permission To Be Great

When I started out, I waited for someone to validate me. I wanted a mentor to say,

"You're ready." I wanted a manager to say, *"You're a natural."*

They didn't. Not at first.

And so I learned to move anyway imperfect, uncertain but willing.

That's the first piece of advice I give any young tech professional: **don't wait for permission. It starts to get messy. Learn loud. Take up space.**

Your voice matters especially if it shakes.

What I Wish Someone Told Me At The Start

1. You don't need to know everything.

You just need to be curious enough to keep learning. Every expert was once a beginner Googling "What is Git?"

2. Soft skills are secret weapons.

Tech will change. People will remember how you made them feel. Kindness, clarity, and consistency will take you further than any programming language.

3. Failure is feedback, not your future.

I once introduced a bug that delayed an entire release. I cried. I apologized. I learned. The key is not perfection, it's bouncing back.

4. Ask questions especially the "dumb" ones.

You're not the only one wondering. The bravest person in the room is the one willing to look confused in pursuit of clarity.

5. Protect your mental health.

Burnout isn't a badge of honor. You deserve boundaries, we all deserve rest and a life outside your screen.

51

Mentorship: Giving What I Never Had

There weren't many people who looked like me when I started: female, introverted, still finding my confidence. That sense of isolation? It cut deep.

So now, I pay it forward.

I mentor software engineers and aspiring tech leaders, not just in tools or techniques, but in truth.

I tell them: *"You're allowed to feel out of place. But you're not alone. And yes you absolutely belong here."*

Sometimes mentorship is a formal session. Sometimes it's a lunch chat. Sometimes it's a single sentence that sticks:

"You don't have to be perfect to be powerful."

Mentorship isn't just passing down knowledge. It's lending courage until someone finds their own.

Real Talk: It's Not Always Easy

There will be moments where you want to quit. Where you compare yourself to others and feel small.

Where the imposter syndrome makes you question every win. But in those moments, please remember this:

You are not behind.
You are not too late.
You are *becoming.*

Keep showing up. That's the difference between those who dream and those who build.

Lessons From The Generation After Me

One of the most humbling things is mentoring someone who ends up teaching *you* something. I've had mentees build apps faster than I did. Ask braver questions. Challenge outdated systems.

They remind me that empowerment is a loop not a ladder. Leadership isn't about pulling others up behind you; it's about lifting as you climb, and then stepping aside when their turn comes to lead. Leadership isn't about pulling others up behind you; it's about lifting as you climb, and then stepping aside when their turn comes to lead.

So if you're young, new or still figuring it out, know this: your fresh eyes are a gift. Your questions are valuable. And your courage to try is leadership in action.

Preparing For The Future

If you're entering tech now, here are truths that will shape your path over the next decade:

1. **AI is your collaborator, not your competitor.**

   Learn how to pair your creativity with machine efficiency. Let AI handle the repetitive; let your humanity drive the meaningful.

2. **Ethics will define your reputation.**

   Tomorrow's leaders will be remembered not just for what they built, but for how responsibly they built it.

3. **Global opportunities will find you.**

   Remote work means your "office" might be spread across three continents. Learn to collaborate across cultures, time zones, and languages.

4. **Resilience will be your edge.**

   Tech will change faster than any of us can predict. Your ability to adapt, relearn, and reinvent will matter more than clinging to one stack.

5. **Community will carry you.**

   Careers aren't solo games anymore. Whether it's an open-source contribution, a local meetup, or a Slack channel, belonging to a tribe will help you thrive.

You Already Have What It Takes

You don't need a fancy title or years of experience to make an impact. You need:

- Grit
- Humility
- Curiosity
- Community
- Willingness to show up even when you are unsure.

And maybe one good mentor.

You've got this.

End of Chapter Reflections:

Pull Quote:

"You don't need to be fearless to lead. You just need to move through fear with purpose."

Journal Prompt:

What advice would you give your younger self when you were first starting out? Now, how can you live by that advice today? How might you offer that wisdom forward to someone just beginning?

Reflection Corner

Bonus Section: Letter to My Younger Self

Dear Younger Me,

You're sitting at your desk right now, probably overthinking every little detail from the syntax of your code to whether you belong in this room at all. You're wondering if you're smart enough, experienced enough or *confident* enough to make it in this field. I know how lonely it feels to be the only woman in the room. I know how exhausting it is to wear a mask of certainty when inside you're full of doubt.

Let me tell you something: you belong.

Not because you have it all figured out. But because you're willing to show up and learn. You think real leaders never get scared, but you'll discover that courage isn't the absence of fear. It's showing up even when you're scared. You think you need to have all the answers, but your greatest power will come from asking the right questions.

You're going to mess up. You're going to feel invisible at times. You'll have moments where you wonder if walking away would be easier. But don't; stay. The version of you I am now is living proof that every late night, every uncomfortable meeting, every brave yes... eventually adds up.

Keep growing. Keep coding. But also, keep listening. Keep caring. One day, your ability to lead from the heart will be the very thing that sets you apart.

Love,

Your Future Self

My Top 10 Leadership Lessons

1. **Listen before you lead.** The loudest voice isn't always the wisest. Leadership starts with deep, active listening.

2. **Imposter syndrome doesn't disqualify you.** Everyone feels like they're faking it at some point. The key is showing up anyway.

3. **You don't need a title to lead.** Influence come from trust and consistency, not your job description.

4. **Vulnerability invites connection.** When you Admit mistakes or ask for help, you give others permission to do the same.

5. **Boundaries protect your brilliance.** Burnout doesn't build legacy. Rest is part of leadership.

6. **Be curious, not controlling.** Great leaders don't micromanage they empower.

7. **Clarity beats charisma.** Fancy speeches fade. Clear communication sticks.

8. **Celebrate small wins.** Momentum builds from acknowledgement, not just achievement.

9. **Feedback is a gift.** Even when it stings, it's an opportunity to grow.

10. **Lead with love, not fear.** Teams don't need Perfect leaders. They need present, caring ones.

Real World Leadership Challenge: Navigating Conflict With Emotional Intelligence and AI

We were in the middle of a high stakes project — multiple teams across time zones, tight deadlines, and one major integration point. The tension was building, especially between two leads who fundamentally disagreed on approach. Standups became icy. Collaboration slowed.

I could've stepped in as a mediator. But I did something different.

First, I asked both individuals to join me for a private async feedback exchange using a shared Notion board giving each of them space to explain their position *without interruption*. Then, I used AI Tools to generate a set of potential solutions from both angles, anonymized the source and brought those into a neutral team workshop.

You know what happened? People stopped defending. They started *building*.

Once they saw their ideas reflected without ego, they reconnected around shared goals. We delivered on time and more importantly, as a stronger, more respected team.

Conflict will never disappear — not in 2025, not in the future, but the way we navigate it will define the kind of leaders we become. Emotional intelligence, curiosity, and even AI can help us turn friction into fuel.

Final Resource Guide: Leadership Tools, Apps & Mindsets

- **Notion** – Team transparency, a sync collaboration, and central documentation
- **AI Tools (OpenAI, Gemini, Claude** – for brainstorming, writing support, decision analysis, retro prompts
- **Slack + Donut** – Culture building through spontaneous pair ups and check ins
- **Miro** – Visual collaboration during retros and planning sessions
- **Loopin** – Meeting summaries, action items, and insight tracking
- **Books:**
  - *Dare to Lead* by Brene Brown
  - *The Fearless Organization* by Amy Edmondson
  - *Radical Candor* by Kim Scott
- **Mindsets to Lead with:**
  - Progress over perfection
  - Listen louder than you speak
  - Create clarity, not control
  - Lead like a coach, not a commander
  - Technology is the tool, *you* are the culture

With these final reflections, I hope this book leaves you not only more equipped but more *encouraged*. Because the truth is, leadership isn't about being fearless. It's about choosing courage again and again in every room, every project, every sprint and every conversation that matters.

This is your time. Build bravely.

Conclusion: Leading With Courage, Purpose & Vision

By now, you've walked through code commits and courageous conversations, through failures that stung and wins that surprised us both. This journey wasn't just about Agile or leadership. It was about learning to choose courage when silence felt safer and learning to keep showing up when fear whispered, *'turn back.'* From keyboard clicks to courageous conversations, from coding in silence to leading with my voice are proof that growth begins long before anyone calls you a leader.

If there's one thing, I want you to remember it's this:

Leadership Isn't A Title. It's A Choice And Often, It's A Scary One.

But fear doesn't disqualify you. In fact, most of the best decisions I've made in my career came *while I was scared.* Scared to speak up. Scared to fail. Scared to be seen.

And I showed up anyway.

That's what *Code and Courage* has always been about, not just my journey into Agile and leadership, but what it took emotionally, mentally and spiritually to stay on the path when everything in me wanted to turn around.

Code gave me structure. Courage gave me strength. And together, they became more than practices — they became a way of leading, living, and showing up. My hope is that as you close these pages, you'll find your own version of "code" to ground you, and your own courage to carry you forward.

The Truth About Becoming A Leader

- I used to think leaders had to have all the answers. Now I know that true leadership is about asking better questions.

- I used to think leaders had to be the loudest in the room. Now I know that strength often looks like listening first.

- I used to think courage meant charging ahead without fear. Now I know courage is walking forward *with fear*, not letting it lead the way.

The Leader I Became

I became a leader not when I got my first Project Manager role... Not when I facilitated my first project...

Not even when I won the Innovation Award (though that moment still gives me chills).

I became a leader the day I decided to lead myself with integrity, consistency, and humility.

When I stopped waiting for someone else to tell me I was enough and started believing it for myself.

And that's what I want for you.

A Note To You — The Reader, The Doer, The Dreamer

If you've ever felt too quiet, too unsure, too "different" to lead know this:

You don't have to become someone else to lead. You have to become *more of who you already are.*

Your empathy is not a weakness. Your mistakes are not your identity. Your growth matters.

Your voice matters.

You matter.

Whether you're in tech, in transition, or simply trying to find your next brave step; this book was written for you.

And if I could leave you with one last whisper of wisdom, it would be this:

- You are allowed to take up space.
- You are allowed to start before you're ready.
- You are allowed to lead with courage even when your hands tremble.

The Work Continues

Agile taught me how to iterate.

Life taught me how to fall and try again. Leadership taught me how to serve.

And now, I pass the torch to you.

The world doesn't need perfect leaders. It needs present people. It needs leaders who are honest, heart led, and human.

So go build. Go lead. And go be brave.

Before You Go...

You've just walked with me through the moments, mistakes, and milestones that shaped my journey into leadership.

But leadership isn't something we only read about it's something we practice, one step, one reflection, and one brave decision at a time.

This bonus section is a collection of tools, reflections, and letters designed to help you take what you've learned and bring it into your own work, your own voice, and your own leadership journey.

Let's go deeper.
Let's go inward.
Let's build forward.

Part I: Leadership Mini-Playbook

1. Courageous Standups

What to ask when people go quiet.

Sometimes, it's not about updates, it's about presence.

I learned to ask:

"What's one thing on your mind before we jump into the board?"

"Who needs support today?"

These questions shift the tone from performance to connection.

2. Tools I Use to Re-center a Burnt-Out Team

When energy dips, I ask:

"What can we let go of?"

"What would make next week feel lighter?"

Then I reprioritize visibly, take the pressure off quietly and bring back joy intentionally.

3. Retros That Heal

Retros should be more than lessons learned. They should be honest. Tender. Safe.

Best question I ever asked:

"What's something you wish someone noticed this sprint but didn't?"

4. Navigating Conflict When You're Still Finding Your Voice

If you're nervous to speak, ask a question first.

"Can I offer a different take?"

"What's the outcome we're both hoping for?"

You don't need to control the room, just soften the tension with curiosity.

5. The "I Don't Know" Power Move

Saying "I'm not sure yet" is not weakness.

It builds trust.

When I don't know, I say:

"Let's figure it out together."

And somehow, we always do.

Part II: Reflective Personal Essays

Leadership Isn't Loud

I used to think leadership meant being the loudest.

But I've learned:

Calm is leadership. So is empathy. So is silence used well.

I lead now not by pushing, but by making space for others to rise.

They didn't listen and I led anyway

I used to feel invisible. Until I realized: my power wasn't in being heard immediately, it was in staying true. I followed through. I kept showing up.

And eventually, the same rooms that ignored me started leaning in.

Part III: Lessons From The Code

1. The Day the Build Failed

Mistakes are not the end, they are part of the process.

In life and leadership, the goal is not perfection. It's ownership, recovery and learning faster.

2. The Power of a Pull Request

The first time I submitted a pull request, I kept refreshing the page, waiting for feedback. What if they hated it? What if I missed something?

But then someone left a comment: "Nice job! Consider abstracting this logic."

It wasn't rejection, it was refinement.

You can grow *and* be good.

Sharing your work is brave. Letting others improve it with you is leadership.

3. Debugging the Human Layer

Sometimes, debugging means starting with empathy. Tech may run on logic, but teams run on trust.

4. Clean Code, Clear Mind

Refactor your life the way you refactor code. Remove clutter, rename what matters, delete what no longer serves.

5. Version Yourself

Code evolves. So do you.

Some days you ship. Some days you rollback. Some days you branch out and explore.

The key is to commit and keep pushing, even if the changes are small.

Part IV: The Reader's Toolkit

Leadership Clarity Map

"You don't have to be fearless to lead. But you do need to know what you stand for."

1. My Top 5 Values: (checklist)
    * Empathy
    * Clarity
    * Integrity
    * Presence
    * Adaptability

2. When I lead, I want people to feel:

Heard, safe, Seen, and motivated.

3. My Affirmation:

"I lead with quiet strength, clear purpose, and open hands."

Retrospective Prompt Pack

* Energy Check-In

"What's your current energy, weather-style?"
"What gave you energy this sprint?"

* Honest Reflection

"What's one thing we're not talking about?"
"Where did we fake alignment?"

* Human-Centered

"Who helped you feel supported this week?"
"Where could we have been kinder?"

- Reset & Repair

"What felt off this sprint?"
"What do we need to leave behind?"

- Looking Forward

"What's one small shift that could change everything?"

Part V: Letters To The Leader I'm Becoming

To the Leader I'm Still Becoming

Dear Me,

You're not there yet. And that's okay.
You still hesitate. You still overthink.
But you keep showing up.
You lead with grace, not noise.
You care. You listen. You stretch.
That's leadership, the kind that doesn't demand a title.
So keep becoming.
Don't rush it.
The version of you you're building will thank you.

Yours,
Me

Part VI: Final Reflection Page

You don't have to arrive to be ready. You just have to move with courage.

You've learned to write code that solves problems, now you're learning to write the kind that transforms people. Let your leadership be like clean code; simple, intentional, and always evolving.

Journal Prompt:

Write a letter to your future self, the one who's lived, led, and grown.

What do you want them to remember about the version of you writing this today?

End of Book Reflections:

Final Pull Quote:

"Courage isn't what comes after fear. It's what you choose to do in the middle of it."

Final Journal Prompt:

If your younger self could see you now, what would they thank you for? What would they ask you to keep fighting for?

Reflection Corner

Letter From The Author:

Code has always been about instructions, logic, and structure. Courage has always been about risk, vulnerability, and stepping into the unknown. At first, they felt like opposites. But over time I realized they belong together.

Because what is leadership if not a living program — one you are constantly rewriting, patching, and upgrading? And what is courage if not the willingness to run the code even when you're not sure it will compile?

Code and Courage isn't just a title. It's the rhythm of building and becoming. One gives you the tools to create. The other gives you the heart to continue.

So as you close this book, I hope you don't see an ending but a version release — *yours*. May you write it with boldness, run it with courage, and keep pushing commits that only you can make. These last pages are your space to reflect, dream and design the leader you're becoming. Use them freely, let them carry your thoughts and let them remind you that your story is still unfolding.

With respect and encourage,

Esther

Reflection Corner

Reflection Corner

Reflection Corner

Reflection Corner

Reflection Corner

Reflection Corner